24 HOUR HISTORY

THE APOLLO 11 MOON LANDING

20 JULY 1969

Nel Yomtov

raintree

Raintree is an imprint of Capstone Global Library
Limited, a company incorporated in England and Wales
having its registered office at 7 Pilgrim Street, London,
EC4V 6LB – Registered company number: 6695582

www.raintreepublishers.co.uk
myorders@raintreepublishers.co.uk

Text © Capstone Global Library Limited 2014
First published in hardback in 2014
Paperback edition first published in 2015
The moral rights of the proprietor have been asserted.

Edited by Adam Miller, Abby Colich, and
    John-Paul Wilkins
Designed by Steve Mead
Original illustrations © Advocate Art 2014
Illustrated by Andrew Chiu
Production by Victoria Fitzgerald
Originated by Capstone Global Library Ltd
Printed and bound in China

ISBN 978 1 406 27362 5 (hardback)
17 16 15 14 13
10 9 8 7 6 5 4 3 2 1

ISBN 978 1 406 27368 7 (paperback)
18 17 16 15
10 9 8 7 6 5 4 3 2 1

A full catalogue record for this book is available from
the British Library.

Acknowledgements
We would like to thank Geza Gyuk for his invaluable
help in the preparation of this book.

CONTENTS

Direct quotations are indicated by a yellow background.

Direct quotations appear on the following pages: 5, 8, 12, 13, 17, 22, 23, 25, 28, 29, 30, 31, 32, 33, 37.

In 1956, the United States and the Soviet Union both announced plans to launch an Earth-orbiting satellite the following year. On 4 October 1957, the Soviets launched the satellite, *Sputnik*.

In January 1958, the Americans sent the *Explorer 1* satellite into low Earth orbit. The Space Race was on.

The Soviets sent the first human into space – Yuri Gagarin – in April 1961.

Meanwhile, the Americans were hard at work on their own space programme.

On 5 May 1961, astronaut Alan Shepard became the first American to travel into space.

Three weeks later, US president John F. Kennedy made an important announcement to Congress.

I believe this nation should commit itself to achieving the goal, before this decade is out, of landing a man on the Moon and returning him safely to the Earth.

Over the following eight years, NASA conducted a series of missions to prepare for a manned moon landing.

Finally, on 16 July 1969, at 9.32 a.m. local time (EDT), *Apollo 11* was launched from the Kennedy Space Center in Florida. Aboard the spacecraft were astronauts Neil Armstrong, Michael Collins, and Edwin "Buzz" Aldrin. Their target: Earth's moon — 384,400 kilometres (238,900 miles) away.

6.20 A.M.

Three hours earlier, the astronauts had left the Manned Spacecraft Operations Building at the Kennedy Space Center. They boarded a van for a short drive to the launch pad.

You boys have a safe flight.

We will. I don't know what we'd do without you, Joe.

Suit technician Joe Schmitt rode with the astronauts, making last-minute checks on their suits.

More than one million eager onlookers gathered on the nearby roads and beaches to watch the historic launch. A worldwide audience of around one billion people followed the action on television.

GOOD LUCK!

GOOD LUCK APOLLO

APOLLO 11

THE MAN BEHIND THE MISSION

Wernher von Braun (1912–1977) was a German-American rocket scientist who developed the *Saturn V* rocket that launched the Apollo missions into space. During World War II (1939–1945), von Braun developed combat rockets for the Nazi regime. In May 1945, he surrendered to American officials. Rather than face trial for aiding the enemy, von Braun agreed to work for the US government. He was brought to the United States to work on its space programme. Von Braun and members of his German rocket team also helped pioneer the development of the two-vehicle Command Module and Lunar Module systems. In 1975, he was awarded the National Medal of Science by the US government.

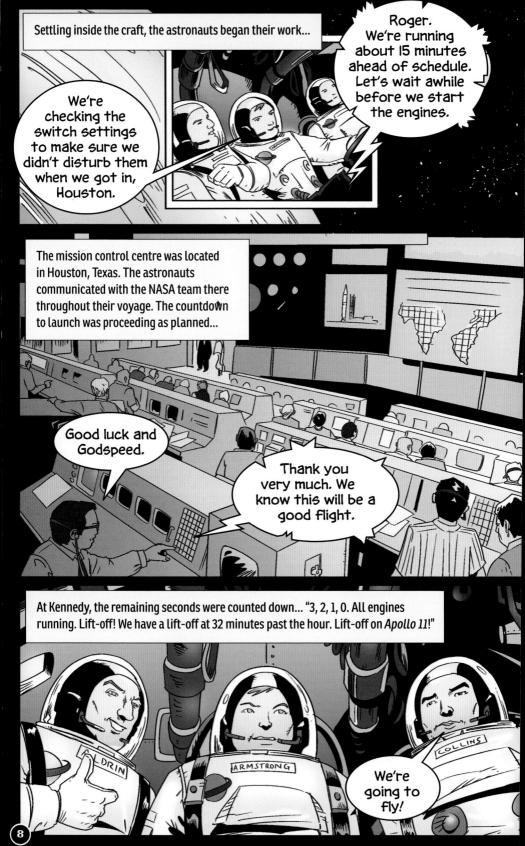

Settling inside the craft, the astronauts began their work...

Roger. We're running about 15 minutes ahead of schedule. Let's wait awhile before we start the engines.

We're checking the switch settings to make sure we didn't disturb them when we got in, Houston.

The mission control centre was located in Houston, Texas. The astronauts communicated with the NASA team there throughout their voyage. The countdown to launch was proceeding as planned...

Good luck and Godspeed.

Thank you very much. We know this will be a good flight.

At Kennedy, the remaining seconds were counted down... "3, 2, 1, 0. All engines running. Lift-off! We have a lift-off at 32 minutes past the hour. Lift-off on *Apollo 11!*"

We're going to fly!

Former president Lyndon B. Johnson and then vice president Spiro Agnew proudly watched the launch from the viewing stand. They were among the thousands of specially invited guests that included Congresspeople, governors, NASA officials, and foreign ministers.

FAST FACT

The Kennedy Space Center is located on Merritt Island, Florida, USA, west of Cape Canaveral on the Atlantic Ocean. It is 55 kilometres (34 miles) long and about 10 kilometres (6 miles) wide, and covers an area of about 570 square kilometres (220 square miles). It has been the launch site for every NASA human spaceflight since 1968.

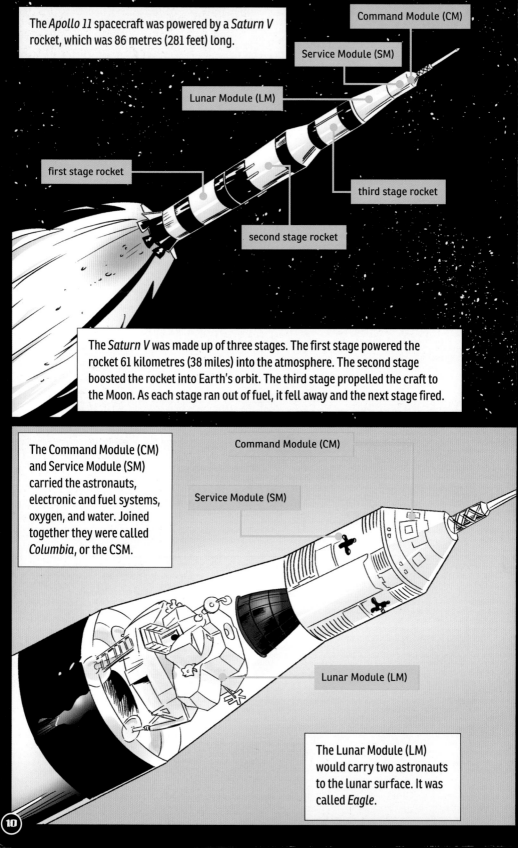

The *Apollo 11* spacecraft was powered by a *Saturn V* rocket, which was 86 metres (281 feet) long.

Command Module (CM)

Service Module (SM)

Lunar Module (LM)

first stage rocket

third stage rocket

second stage rocket

The *Saturn V* was made up of three stages. The first stage powered the rocket 61 kilometres (38 miles) into the atmosphere. The second stage boosted the rocket into Earth's orbit. The third stage propelled the craft to the Moon. As each stage ran out of fuel, it fell away and the next stage fired.

The Command Module (CM) and Service Module (SM) carried the astronauts, electronic and fuel systems, oxygen, and water. Joined together they were called *Columbia*, or the CSM.

Command Module (CM)

Service Module (SM)

Lunar Module (LM)

The Lunar Module (LM) would carry two astronauts to the lunar surface. It was called *Eagle*.

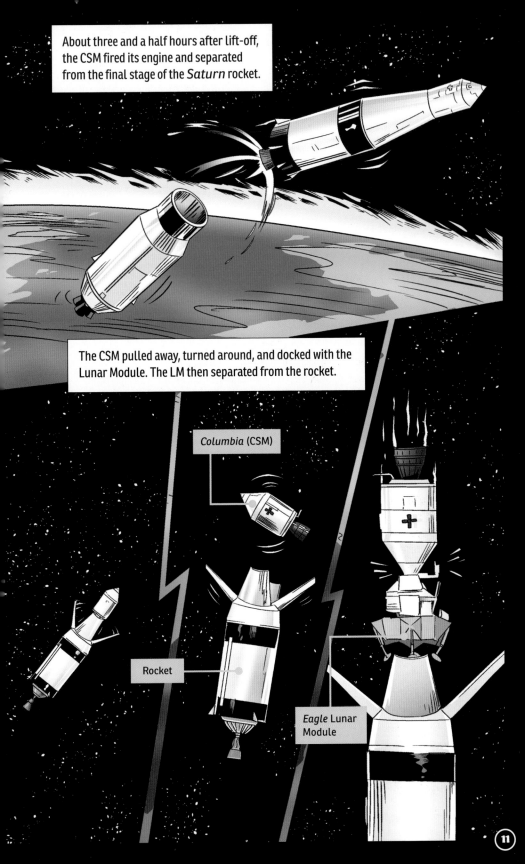

About three and a half hours after lift-off, the CSM fired its engine and separated from the final stage of the *Saturn* rocket.

The CSM pulled away, turned around, and docked with the Lunar Module. The LM then separated from the rocket.

Columbia (CSM)

Rocket

Eagle Lunar Module

19 July. When *Apollo 11* flew around the far side of the Moon, it was temporarily out of communication with Mission Control.

The engines slowed down the spacecraft and allowed the Moon's gravity to "grab" the ship.

Starting engine burn for Moon approach.

You guys should get a good night's sleep before going into the LM.

Now in the Moon's orbit, the astronauts finished off some chores and ate supper. They dined on tuna salad, chicken stew, and butterscotch pudding.

Sounds good, Mike.

If tomorrow and the next day are like today, we'll be safe.

WHAT'S FOR DINNER?

The crew of *Apollo 11* had more than 70 choices of food on their menu. Many of the items were freeze-dried and could be eaten after adding water. Others were kept wet in plastic packs. Among the selection were beef and potatoes, tuna salad, and hot dogs. Beverages included orange drink, grape punch, and cocoa. The dessert menu included fruit cake, banana pudding, and brownies.

20 July 10.02 A.M.

Thanks for helping us suit up, Mike. Give us a couple of minutes to settle in.

After eating breakfast, Armstrong and Aldrin moved from *Columbia* into the lunar module, *Eagle*.

The clock in *Eagle* had to be set to match the clock in *Columbia*.

I have 097.03.30 set in.

Got it!

Fifteeen seconds to go. 10...5, 4, 3, 2, 1. Mark.

Charles Duke, capsule communicator at Mission Control, had to make sure that *Eagle* and *Columbia* were able to communicate with each other. After Collins sealed the hatch between the two modules, Duke spoke.

Columbia, Houston. Do you read?

Eagle, do you read Columbia?

Loud and clear.

Yes.

Then you're "go" for undocking.

Understood, Houston.

With Houston's permission, *Eagle* and *Columbia* were ready to separate.

SEA OF TRANQUILLITY

The site where *Apollo 11* landed is called the Sea of Tranquillity. This is translated from its Latin name *Mare Tranquillitatis*. Italian astronomers Francesco Grimaldi and Giovanni Riccioli named the site in 1651. The Sea of Tranquillity is not a sea of water. In fact, it is a large, dark, rocky plain that was formed by volcanic eruptions. The area has a bluish colour due to the metal in the soil and in the rocks, which are made of basalt.

Moments after firing the rockets...

Program alarm. It's a 12-02, Houston.

Neither astronaut had seen this alarm during their months of testing and training. But they both knew that some alarms meant that the mission had to be called off.

But Houston urged the astronauts to push on...

FAST FACT
The computers on board *Apollo 11* had less processing power than a modern-day mobile phone.

We've seen this before. As long as it doesn't happen again, we'll be fine.

The astronauts breathed a sigh of relief. They were now only 6,400 metres (21,000 feet) from the Moon's surface.

Shutdown!

Houston, Tranquility Base here. The *Eagle* has landed.

3.17 P.M.

On 20 July 1969, humanity's greatest dream had come true: humans had landed on the Moon.

You got a bunch of guys about to turn blue. We're breathing again. Thanks a lot.

FAST FACT

It is estimated that more than 40,000 engineers, scientists, and technicians from more than 20,000 companies and universities worked on the Apollo space programme.

As he orbited the Moon, Collins was delighted to hear that his friends had landed safely.

It sure sounded great from up here. You guys did a fantastic job!

Thank you. Just keep that orbiting base ready for us up there now.

Will do.

Before the astronauts prepared for their extravehicular activity (EVA), Aldrin spoke...

I'd like to take this opportunity to ask every person listening in, whoever and wherever they may be, to pause for a moment and contemplate the events of the past few hours and to give thanks in his or her own way.

For the next seven hours, the astronauts ran through the long checklist of equipment they needed to venture out onto the lunar surface. When they were finished, they helped each other into their bulky spacesuits.

Armstrong opened a hatch that exposed a television camera. The camera would show people around the world the historic moonwalk.

Meanwhile, *Columbia* orbited on the other side of the Moon. Out of communication range, Collins would be unable to hear Armstrong as he stepped onto the lunar surface.

In his spacesuit, Armstrong prepared to exit *Eagle*.

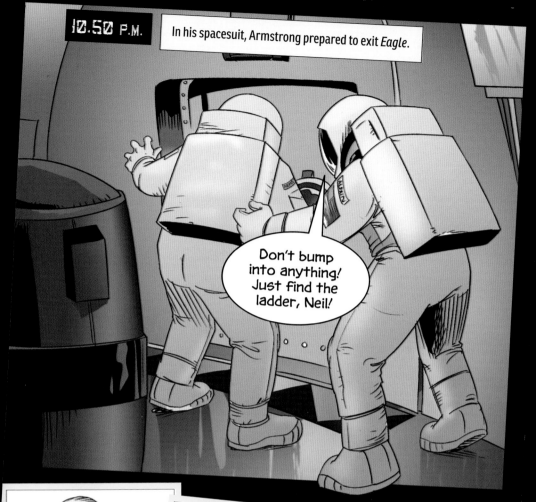

Don't bump into anything! Just find the ladder, Neil!

EXTRAVEHICULAR SPACESUIT

The astronauts wore a spacesuit known as the Extravehicular Mobility Unit (EMU) on their moonwalk. The suit weighed 83 kilograms (183 pounds) and provided enough oxygen for a four-hour mission on the lunar surface. The helmet was equipped with two visors that offered temperature control and protection against small meteors and dangerous ultraviolet light. Communication between the astronauts and Mission Control was made possible by "Snoopy hats". These devices fit over the astronauts' head and ears, and contained microphones and earphones. They were worn under the helmet.

10.56 P.M.

I'm going to step off the LM now.

FAST FACT

Armstrong's "one small step" wasn't actually that small. He had landed *Eagle* so gently that its shock absorbers didn't fully close. He had to hop 1.1 metres (3.5 feet) from the *Eagle*'s ladder to the surface!

On 20 July 1969, Neil Armstrong became the first human to set foot on the Moon.

That's one small step for [a] man...

...one giant leap for mankind.

Millions of people around the world witnessed Armstrong's first step on the Moon.

Mum! This is so exciting!

Thanks for letting me stay up late! I wouldn't miss this for anything!

11.09 P.M.

The surface is fine and powdery.... I can pick it up loosely with my toe.

After snapping a few pictures with a camera attached to his chest, Armstrong gathered contingency samples.

These soil and rock samples were taken early in the moonwalk in case the astronauts had to lift off right away or were unable to collect them later.

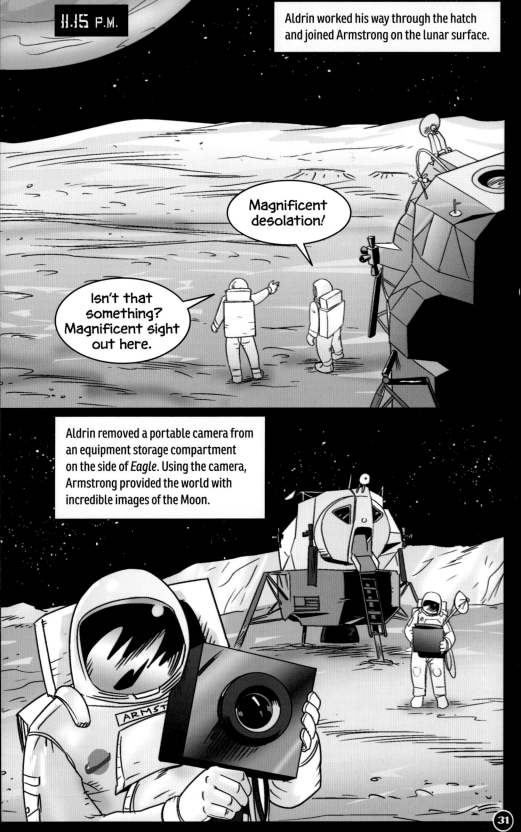

Aldrin's next assignment was to test the Moon's gravity. On the lunar surface, he weighed only one-sixth of his weight on Earth. Aldrin joyfully became the first human to do the "kangaroo hop"!

Watching TV back on Earth, Aldrin's wife, Jean, laughed so hard that she cried.

The astronauts then received an important phone call from President Nixon.

11.48 P.M.

Hello, Neil and Buzz, I'm talking to you by telephone from the Oval Room at the White House....For every American, this has to be the proudest day of our lives....Thank you very much.

FAST FACT

President Nixon had a speech ready in case the astronauts missed being picked up by the orbiting Command Module. It read, "These brave men, Neil Armstrong and Edwin Aldrin, know that there is no hope for their recovery. But they also know that there is hope for mankind in their sacrifice."

As Armstrong returned to collecting a large sample of lunar rocks...

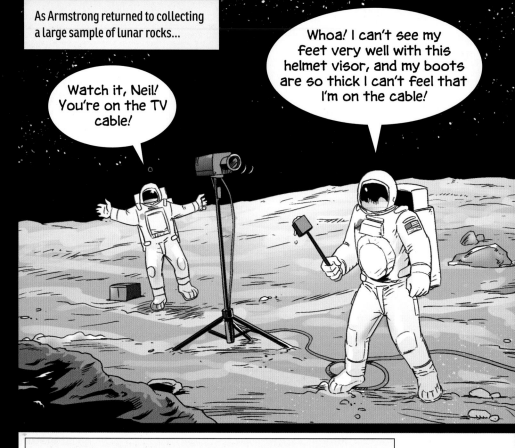

Watch it, Neil! You're on the TV cable!

Whoa! I can't see my feet very well with this helmet visor, and my boots are so thick I can't feel that I'm on the cable!

Aldrin took a photo of the imprint his boot made in the lunar surface. It has become one of the most famous photos in history. Then he snapped shots of *Eagle* to show NASA engineers the condition of the craft.

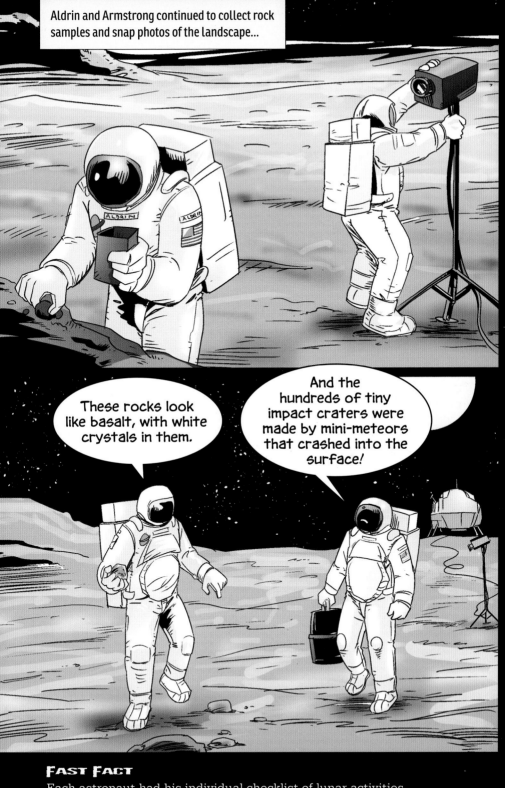

NASA had decided to allow 30 minutes for rock sampling, but things were going slower than planned. With time running out, Armstrong noticed a crater about 61 metres (200 feet) away from *Eagle*. He quickly set off for it with his camera.

I'd love to get down there for a rock sample, but I have to get back. Maybe next time...

Buzz, Houston. It's time for you to end your EVA*.

Roger, Houston.

I'm picking up some really good samples of rock now.

Roger. Then it's time to head up the ladder.

*Extravehicular activity. This refers to any activity done outside the spacecraft in space.

11.11 A.M. 21 July. Once back in *Eagle*, Aldrin closed its hatch and reported to Houston that mankind's historic walk on the Moon was officially over.

That's a real great day, guys. I really enjoyed it.

Thank you. You couldn't have enjoyed it as much as we did!

The astronauts took many rock and soil samples from the Moon's surface. But they also left something behind: a stainless steel plaque to commemorate humanity's greatest triumph.

HERE MEN FROM THE PLANET EARTH FIRST SET FOOT UPON THE MOON JULY 1969, A.D.
WE CAME IN PEACE FOR ALL MANKIND

The voyage of *Apollo 11* inspired people around the world more than 40 years ago, and it continues to inspire us today. It teaches us that any dream is worth chasing and anything we work for can be accomplished.

THE LEGACY OF APOLLO 11

After re-entering *Eagle*, Armstrong and Aldrin remained on the Moon's surface in the LM for ten more hours. Finally, on 21 July at 1.54 p.m., *Eagle* blasted off from the lunar surface to begin redocking operations with Collins, who was still orbiting the Moon in *Columbia*. At 12.50 p.m. on 24 July, the Command Module, the only part of the spacecraft to return through Earth's atmosphere, splashed down in the Pacific Ocean. The spacecraft – carrying three tired but cheerful and grateful astronauts – was recovered by the aircraft carrier USS *Hornet* minutes later.

Armstrong walked on the Moon for a total of 2 hours, 37 minutes and 37 seconds, and Aldrin for around 40 minutes less. Yet the legacy of *Apollo 11*'s crew – Armstrong, Aldrin, and Collins – will be felt for many generations to come. By making President Kennedy's dream a reality, the world viewed the United States as a more scientifically advanced nation than its rival, the Soviet Union. The successful landing also demonstrated the United States' technological and engineering prowess to other countries all around the world.

The Apollo missions rapidly sped up the pace of technology development, especially in the United States. The technology used to put Americans into space was used to develop computer hardware and software, robotics, national defence, methods of transport, food processing, and improvements in health care.

Thousands of everyday products originated from space programme technology, including fabrics for clothing and shoes, cordless power tools, and lighting systems. The internet also owes a huge thanks to the space programme.

Apollo 11's success encouraged many nations to begin their own space programmes. Since 1969, France, Korea, Poland, Iran, China, Bulgaria, and many countries have founded their own space agencies. The International Space Station (ISS), the most complex international scientific project in history, is another example of *Apollo 11*'s far-reaching legacy.

Many people around the world still consider *Apollo 11* the greatest achievement of the 20th century. We will always remember that moment not only for humans setting foot on the Moon, but also for leaving planet Earth in search of a new and promising future.

TIMELINE

4 October 1957	Soviets launch *Sputnik* satellite
3 November 1957	Laika, a Russian dog on board *Sputnik 2*, becomes the first animal to orbit Earth
12 April 1961	Soviets send a human into space for the first time
5 May 1961	Alan Shepard becomes the first American to travel into space
25 May 1961	President John F. Kennedy urges the United States to land a man on the Moon "before this decade is out"
1961–1969	United States conducts numerous space projects, including the Mercury, Gemini, and Apollo missions
22 November 1963	President Kennedy is assassinated in Dallas, Texas
16 July 1969, 9.32 a.m.	*Apollo 11* launches from Kennedy Space Center in Florida
20 July, 10.02 a.m.	Aldrin and Armstrong move from *Columbia* Command Module to *Eagle* Lunar Module to prepare for undocking
12.44 p.m.	*Columbia* and *Eagle* complete successful undocking
2.08 p.m.	*Eagle* prepares for powered descent
3.17 p.m.	*Eagle* lands on lunar surface
10.50 p.m.	Armstrong prepares to exit *Eagle*
10.56 p.m.	Armstrong becomes first human to step on the Moon
11.09 p.m.	Armstrong collects contingency samples
11.15 p.m.	Aldrin joins Armstrong on lunar surface
11.41 p.m.	Astronauts plant American flag on Moon surface
11.48 p.m.	President Richard Nixon speaks to Armstrong and Aldrin
21 July, 1.11 a.m.	Hatch to *Eagle* is shut; moonwalk officially ends
1.54 p.m.	*Eagle* blasts off from lunar surface
24 July, 12.50 p.m.	Command Module carrying Armstrong, Aldrin, and Collins splashes down in the Pacific Ocean

MAP OF COMMAND MODULE SPLASHDOWN

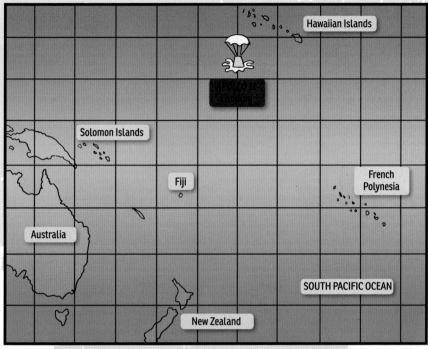

Hawaiian Islands

Solomon Islands

Fiji

French Polynesia

Australia

SOUTH PACIFIC OCEAN

New Zealand

CAST OF CHARACTERS

Lyndon B. Johnson (1908–1973)
Johnson was the 36th president of the United States. LBJ, as he was commonly known, took office upon John F. Kennedy's assassination in 1963. Johnson believed a successful Moon launch would be a great contribution to America's image around the world. Much of Apollo's research and development came during his time in office, from 1963 to 1969.

Richard M. Nixon (1913–1994)
Nixon was the 37th president of the United States and held office at the time of the *Apollo 11* Moon landing. He believed the US space programme was important for exploration, to gain scientific knowledge, and to apply the lessons learned in space to benefit people on Earth. He watched the Moon landing from his office and spoke to Armstrong and Aldrin shortly after they stepped onto the lunar surface. Nixon called his conversation with the astronauts "the most historic telephone call ever made from the White House".

John F. Kennedy (1917–1963)
Kennedy was the 35th president of the United States. He was determined that the United States should defeat the Soviet Union in the Space Race. In May 1961, he urged Congress to support the goal of landing a man on the Moon and returning him safely to Earth within the decade of the 1960s. He was assassinated in Dallas, Texas, on 22 November 1963, less than three years into his term in office.

Edwin "Buzz" Aldrin Jr (b. 1930)
Aldrin was a pilot in the US Air Force and became an astronaut in 1963. In 1966, he orbited Earth aboard the *Gemini 12* spacecraft, where he performed both docking operations with another space vehicle and extravehicular activities (EVAs). Because of his expertise in this area, he was chosen as a member of the Apollo crew and became the second human to set foot on the Moon. He retired from the Air Force in 1972 and wrote two books about his activities in the space programme, *Return to Earth* and *Men from Earth*.

Neil Armstrong (1930–2012)
Armstrong was a US Navy pilot, and joined the National Advisory Committee for Aeronautics (NACA) in 1952, which was later replaced by the National Aeronautics and Space Administration (NASA). He became an astronaut in 1962 and flew his first space mission as commander of *Gemini 8* in 1966. As commander of *Apollo 11*, he became the first person to step on the Moon. He briefly served as deputy associate administrator for aeronautics at NASA headquarters, where he was responsible for the coordination and management of research and technology. He left NASA in 1971 to teach and to act as spokesperson for several different businesses.

Michael Collins (b. 1930)
Collins was a fighter pilot and experimental test pilot in the US Air Force. In 1963, he became a NASA astronaut and piloted the three-day *Gemini 10* mission in 1966. His second flight was as Command Module pilot aboard *Apollo 11*. He remained in the Moon's orbit while Armstrong and Aldrin landed and walked on the lunar surface. After retiring from NASA in 1970, he briefly held a position in the US Department of State as assistant secretary of state for public affairs. The following year, he joined the Smithsonian Institution as the director of the National Air and Space Museum, where he was responsible for the construction of the new museum building in Washington, D.C.

Charles Moss Duke Jr (b. 1935)
Duke was a brigadier general in the US Air Force and a NASA astronaut. As lunar module pilot for *Apollo 16* in 1972, he became the tenth person to walk on the Moon. He served as capsule communicator (CAPCOM) on the *Apollo 11* launch, and was the voice of Mission Control in Houston, Texas, speaking to the astronauts during their historic voyage.

GLOSSARY

basalt hard, dense, dark rock formed by volcanic action

commemorate honour and remember an important event or person

contemplate think about something

contingency event that may occur but is not likely or intended; a possibility

crater large hole in the ground caused by something falling or exploding, such as a meteorite or a bomb

descent move from a higher to a lower place

desolation complete emptiness

Gemini second human US spaceflight programme whose goal was to develop space travel techniques for the Apollo programme of landing a man on the Moon

Mercury first US spaceflight programme, which sent the first American into space

meteor piece of rock or metal in space that speeds into a heavenly body's atmosphere and forms a light as it burns and falls

National Aeronautics and Space Administration (NASA) US government agency that is responsible for the space programme

satellite spacecraft that is sent into orbit around Earth, the Moon, or another celestial body

ultraviolet invisible radiation wavelengths that can be harmful to living things

venture go somewhere or do something daring, dangerous, or unpleasant

FIND OUT MORE

Books

Exploring Space (Sci-Hi), Robert Snedden (Raintree, 2010)

Moon (Eyewitness) (Dorling Kindersley, 2011)

The Moon (Astronaut Travel Guides), Chris Oxlade
    (Raintree, 2013)

Moonshot: The Flight of Apollo 11, Brian Floca (Atheneum
    Books, 2009)

What Does Space Exploration Do for Us? (Earth, Space, and
    Beyond), Neil Morris (Raintree, 2012)

DVDs

Moonwalk One – The Director's Cut (The Attic Room Ltd, 2009)

The Sky at Night – Apollo 11 (Acorn, 2009)

In the Shadow of the Moon (Channel 4 DVD, 2008)

From the Earth to the Moon – The Signature Edition
    (Warner Home Video, 2006)

Websites

www.bbc.co.uk/science/space/solarsystem/space_missions
Find out about *Apollo 11* and many other space missions on this
website from the BBC.

www.firstmenonthemoon.com
Relive the *Apollo 11* Moon landing, with real video and audio
footage, images, transcripts, and much more.

news.nationalgeographic.com/news/2009/07/090715-moon
-landing-apollo-facts.html
This site offers facts and figures on *Apollo 11*'s historic flight.

science.nasa.gov/science-news/science-at-nasa/2006/19jul
_seaoftranquillity
This site features the official NASA retelling of the Moon landing
and links to photo galleries.

Places to visit

National Space Centre

Exploration Drive
Leicester
LE4 5NS
0845 605 2001
www.spacecentre.co.uk
The National Space Centre is the UK's largest space attraction, and offers plenty for all the family. Popular attractions include the UK's largest planetarium, a 3-D simulator ride, interactive galleries, and much more.

If you are ever in the United States, you could visit one of these historic sites, which played key roles in the *Apollo 11* mission.

Kennedy Space Center

SR 405
Kennedy Space Center, FL 32899
www.kennedyspacecenter.com
Stand under the massive rockets that put NASA astronauts into space, train in spaceflight simulators, explore space history exhibits, meet an astronaut, and even view a launch.

Space Center Houston

1601 NASA Parkway
Houston, TX 77058
www.spacecenter.org
The official visitors centre for NASA's Johnson Space Center offers hands-on exhibits, a tour of the historic Mission Control Center, a gallery of spacesuits dating back to the 1960s, and much more.

INDEX